Junior Drug Awareness
Alcohol

Junior Drug Awareness

Alcohol

Amphetamines and Other Uppers

Crack and Cocaine

Ecstasy and Other Designer Drugs

Heroin

How to Get Help

How to Say No

Inhalants and Solvents

LSD, PCP, and Other Hallucinogens

Marijuana

Nicotine and Cigarettes

Pain Relievers, Diet Pills, and
    Other Over-the-Counter Drugs

Prozac and Other Antidepressants

Steroids

Valium and Other Downers

Junior Drug Awareness

Alcohol

Introduction by **BARRY R. McCAFFREY**
Director, Office of National Drug Control Policy

Foreword by **STEVEN L. JAFFE, M.D.**
Senior Consulting Editor,
Professor of Child and Adolescent Psychiatry, Emory University

Nancy B. Peacock

Chelsea House Publishers
Philadelphia

CHELSEA HOUSE PUBLISHERS
Editor in Chief Stephen Reginald
Production Manager Pamela Loos
Director of Photography Judy L. Hasday
Art Director Sara Davis
Managing Editor James D. Gallagher
Senior Production Editor LeeAnne Gelletly

Staff for ALCOHOL
Senior Editor Therese De Angelis
Contributing Editors John Ziff, James D. Gallagher
Editorial Assistant Jessica Carey
Associate Art Director Takeshi Takahashi
Picture Researcher Sandy Jones
Cover Designer Takeshi Takahashi

Cover Photo ©1997 Charles Gupton/The Stock Market

The Chelsea House World Wide Website address is
http://www.chelseahouse.com

3 5 7 9 8 6 4 2

Peacock, Nancy.
Alcohol / Nancy Peacock; introduction by Barry R.
McCaffrey.
    pp. cm. — (Junior drug awareness)
Includes bibliographical references.
Summary: Describes the effect of alcohol on the body,
the reasons why people use it, the dangers of abusing it,
and methods of treatment, and the prevention of addic-
tion.
ISBN 0-7910-5174-9 (hc)
1. High school students—Alcohol use—United States—
Juvenile literature. 2. Drinking of alcoholic beverages—
United States—Juvenile literature. 3. Alcoholism—
United States—Prevention—Juvenile literature. [1.
Alcohol. 2. Alcoholism.] I. Title. II. Series.
HV5824.Y68P43 1999
362.292—dc21   99-22438
                                                     CIP

CONTENTS

Staying Away from Illegal Drugs,   6
    Tobacco Products, and Alcohol
Barry R. McCaffrey

Why Should I Learn About Drugs?   10
Steven L. Jaffe, M.D.

1 Alcoholism and Alcohol Abuse   13

2 Alcohol Throughout History   27

3 Alcohol's Effects on the Body   35

4 Why Do People Use Alcohol?   45

5 Underage Drinking   55

6 Where Do You Go From Here?   65

Glossary   72

Bibliography   74

Find Out More About Alcohol
    and Other Drug Abuse   75

Index   78

by Barry R. McCaffrey
Director, Office of National
Drug Control Policy

STAYING AWAY FROM ILLEGAL DRUGS, TOBACCO PRODUCTS, AND ALCOHOL

Good health allows you to be as strong, happy, smart, and skillful as you can possibly be. The worst thing about illegal drugs is that they damage people from the inside. Our bodies and minds are wonderful, complicated systems that run like finely tuned machines when we take care of ourselves.

Doctors prescribe legal drugs, called medicines, to heal us when we become sick, but dangerous chemicals that are not recommended by doctors, nurses, or pharmacists are called illegal drugs. These drugs cannot be bought in stores because they harm different organs of the body, causing illness or even death. Illegal drugs, such as marijuana, cocaine or "crack," heroin, methamphetamine ("meth"), and other dangerous substances are against the law because they affect our ability to think, work, play, sleep, or eat.

If anyone ever offers you illegal drugs or any kind of pills, liquids, substances to smoke, or shots to inject into your body, tell them you're not interested. You should report drug pushers—people who distribute these poisons—to parents, teachers, police, coaches, clergy, or other adults whom you trust.

Cigarettes and alcohol are also illegal for youngsters. Tobacco products and drinks like wine, beer, and liquor are particularly harmful for children and teenagers because their bodies, especially their nervous systems, are still developing. For this reason, young people are more likely to be hurt by illicit drugs—including cigarettes and alcohol. These two products kill more people—from cancer, and automobile accidents caused by intoxicated drivers—than all other drugs combined. We say about drug use: "Users are losers." Be a winner and stay away from illegal drugs, tobacco products, and alcoholic beverages.

Here are four reasons why you shouldn't use illegal drugs:

- Illegal drugs can cause brain damage.
- Illegal drugs are "psychoactive." This means that they change your personality or the way you feel. They also impair your judgment. While under the influence of drugs, you are more likely to endanger your life or someone else's. You will also be less able to protect yourself from danger.
- Many illegal drugs are addictive, which means that once a person starts taking them, stopping is extremely difficult. An addict's body craves the drug and becomes dependent upon it. The illegal drug–user may become sick if the drug is discontinued and so may become a slave to drugs.

- Some drugs, called "gateway" substances, can lead a person to take more-dangerous drugs. For example, a 12-year-old who smokes marijuana is 79 times more likely to have an addiction problem later in life than a child who never tries marijuana.

Here are some reasons why you shouldn't drink alcoholic beverages, including beer and wine coolers:

- Alcohol is the second leading cause of death in our country. More than 100,000 people die every year because of drinking.
- Adolescents are twice as likely as adults to be involved in fatal alcohol-related car crashes.
- Half of all assaults against girls or women involve alcohol.
- Drinking is illegal if you are under the age of 21. You could be arrested for this crime.

Here are three reasons why you shouldn't smoke cigarettes:

- Nicotine is highly addictive. Once you start smoking, it is very hard to stop, and smoking cigarettes causes lung cancer and other diseases. Tobacco- and nicotine-related diseases kill more than 400,000 people every year.
- Each day, 3,000 kids begin smoking. One-third of these youngsters will probably have their lives shortened because of tobacco use.
- Children who smoke cigarettes are almost six times more likely to use other illegal drugs than kids who don't smoke.

If your parents haven't told you how they feel about the dangers of illegal drugs, ask them. One of every 10 kids aged 12 to 17 is using illegal drugs. They do not understand the risks they are taking with their health and their lives. However, the vast majority of young people in America are smart enough to figure out that drugs, cigarettes, and alcohol could rob them of their future. Be your body's best friend: guard your mental and physical health by staying away from drugs.

WHY SHOULD I LEARN ABOUT DRUGS?

Steven L. Jaffe, M.D., Senior Consulting Editor,
Professor of Child and Adolescent Psychiatry,
Emory University

Your grandparents and great-grandparents did not think much about "drug awareness." That's because drugs, to most of them, simply meant "medicine."

Of the three types of drugs, medicine is the good type. Medicines such as penicillin and aspirin promote healing and help sick people get better.

Another type of drug is obviously bad for you because it is poison. Then there are the kinds of drugs that fool you, such as marijuana and LSD. They make you feel good, but they harm your body and brain.

Our great crisis today is that this third category of drugs has become widely abused. Drugs of abuse are everywhere, not just in rough neighborhoods. Many teens are introduced to drugs by older brothers, sisters, friends, or even friends' parents. Some people may use only a little bit of a drug, but others who inherited a tendency to become addicted may move on to using drugs all the time. If a family member is or was an alcoholic or an addict, a young person is at greater risk of becoming one.

Drug abuse can weaken us physically. Worse, it can cause permanent mental damage. Our brain is the most important part of our body. Our thoughts, hopes, wishes, feelings, and memories are located there, within 100 billion nerve cells. Alcohol and drugs that are abused will harm—and even destroy—these cells. During the teen years, your brain continues to develop and grow, but drugs and alcohol can impair this growth.

I treat all types of teenagers at my hospital programs and in my office. Many suffer from depression or anxiety. A lot of them abuse drugs and alcohol, and this makes their depression or fears worse. I have celebrated birthdays and high school graduations with many of my patients. But I have also been to sad funerals for others who have died from problems with drug abuse.

Doctors understand more about drugs today than ever before. We've learned that some substances (even some foods) that we once thought were harmless can actually cause health problems. And for some people, medicines that help relieve one symptom might cause problems in other ways. This is because each person's body chemistry and immune system are different.

For all of these reasons, drug awareness is important for everyone. We need to learn which drugs to avoid or question— not only the destructive, illegal drugs we hear so much about in the news, but also ordinary medicines we buy at the supermarket or pharmacy. We need to understand that even "good" drugs can hurt us if they are not used correctly. We also need accurate scientific knowledge, not just rumors we hear from other teens.

Drug awareness enables you to make good decisions. It allows you to become powerful and strong and have a meaningful life!

Each year, thousands of people in the United States see their lives swirling away as they pour themselves another drink. They are alcoholics—people who have become addicted to alcohol. But alcoholics are not the only people with drinking problems. One 1997 survey estimated that about 11.2 million Americans are "heavy drinkers," meaning they consume five or more drinks on the same occasion more than five times a month.

ALCOHOLISM AND ALCOHOL ABUSE

"I started drinking with friends when I slept over at their houses. Just sneaking a drink here, a beer there. After a while, though, drinking became the only way I thought I could have fun. Only I didn't drink to have fun. I drank to get drunk."

Actress Drew Barrymore was six years old when she starred in the movie *E.T.* She was only 10 years old when she became addicted to alcohol. In her autobiography, *Little Girl Lost,* Drew describes how alcohol became a way to avoid the sadness in her life. "Instead of dealing with whatever pain or troubles you have," she says, "you medicate them. The problems are still there, you just don't feel them until the drug or alcohol wears off. Then you medicate again. That's the cycle I was entering. When I felt pain, I medicated it."

George McGovern was the 1972 Democratic nominee

for president of the United States and a former U.S. senator from South Dakota. He became a victim of **alcoholism** when his alcoholic daughter, Terry, froze to death in a snowdrift in 1995. "Alcoholism is like a thief in the night," McGovern said. "It can steal up on you and seize your life, liberty, and pursuit of happiness before you comprehend what has happened." In memory of his daughter and to warn others about the dangers of alcohol abuse, McGovern wrote a book about the tragedy, called *Terry: My Daughter's Life-and-Death Struggle with Alcoholism.* In it he wrote:

> Every day three hundred Americans die quietly of alcoholism. Many of them go unnoticed. Some of them have been out of touch with their families for years. There might be a small news item reporting that the police have found an unidentified body in a park or on a street or in a cheap rooming house— or in a snowbank. These people are usually not the subject of public notice or concern. But each one of them is a precious soul who was once a little girl or boy filled with promise and dreams. They are the silent victims of the nation's number one health problem—alcoholism.

McGovern describes the sadness, pain, anger, and guilt that families feel when a loved one struggles with alcoholism: "How could this have happened? My lovable little girl who had given me ten thousand laughs, countless moments of affection and joy, and, yes, years of anxiety and disappointment—now frozen to death like some deserted outcast? The blunt answer is that Teresa

Actress Drew Barrymore takes a drink—of soda—while discussing a movie project in 1998. The star of such hit movies as *E.T.* and *The Wedding Singer*, Drew became addicted to alcohol when she was only 10 years old.

Jane McGovern was an alcoholic—one of twenty million alcoholics in the United States."

Alcohol is the most widely used drug in the United States. About 100,000 Americans die every year from alcohol-related causes. Only smoking and an unhealthy lifestyle—poor diet with lack of exercise—cause more preventable deaths. In addition, more than 76 million Americans have experienced alcoholism in a member of their families. More than half of all Americans say that at least one of their close relatives has a drinking problem.

What Is Alcoholism?

The National Institute on Alcohol Abuse and Alcoholism (NIAAA) was created by the federal government in 1970 to supervise funds for research on alcoholism. In 1999 the U.S. government budgeted more than $230 million to search for ways to prevent and treat alcoholism.

According to the NIAAA, alcoholism is a disease, and is characterized by these symptoms:

- **Craving**—A person feels a strong need to drink.
- Loss of control—After a person starts drinking, he or she cannot stop doing so.
- **Tolerance**—The person needs increasing amounts of the drug to achieve the same level of **intoxication** (drunkenness).
- **Physical dependence** (also called **addiction**)—the person's body has become dependent on alcohol to function normally. Stopping the drug causes **withdrawal** symptoms, such as nausea, sweating, tremors, and intense anxiety. These symptoms are relieved only when the person drinks more alcohol or takes a **minor tranquilizer.**

Alcohol Abuse

Does this mean that everyone who drinks too much is an alcoholic? Although there are no clear boundaries separating different categories of drinking, the NIAAA has also described a second pattern of alcohol consumption known as **alcohol abuse.** Alcohol abuse is a pattern of drinking that causes one or more of these things to happen within a year:

- The person is not able to perform normal tasks at home, school, or work.
- The person drinks while driving a car or doing something else that should never be done while drinking.
- The person is arrested for driving while intoxicated or hurts someone while intoxicated.
- The person continues to drink even though it harms family relationships and friendships.

How Much and How Often?

How often and *when* a person drinks alcohol is as important as how much alcohol he or she drinks. For example, one drink every day—seven drinks each week—is considered drinking in **moderation** (drinking in small amounts) for an adult. However, drinking seven drinks in one night is considered alcohol abuse.

For people who drink alcohol, the safest way to enjoy it is in moderation. Most people agree that moderate drinking is drinking that doesn't cause problems for the drinker or others. But that definition has different meanings for different people.

Safe drinking limits vary from person to person. The U.S. Department of Agriculture and the U.S. Department of Health and Human Services state this general rule: moderate drinking means no more than two drinks a day for most men and no more than one drink a day for most women.

Why are there different limits for men and women? Scientists have discovered that men have more of a specific **enzyme** (a special kind of protein) known as **alcohol dehydrogenase** (**ADH**) in the lining of the stomach. ADH converts alcohol into a substance called acetaldehyde, which is then changed to acetic acid. The body then converts acetic acid into carbon dioxide and water.

The Pros and Cons
of Moderate Drinking

There are some benefits to drinking moderately. Low doses of alcohol can make a person feel more relaxed, less nervous or anxious, and even more friendly. But medical experts are not sure whether these effects are physical, meaning they are produced by the alcohol itself, or psychological, meaning that a person consuming alcohol simply expects to feel better. Moderate alcohol consumption may also lower one's risk of death from diseases that affect the arteries of the heart. Some elderly people also claim that their appetites and moods improve when they drink small amounts of alcohol each day.

But moderate drinking has risks, too. Alcohol can decrease the risk of having certain kinds of **strokes** (sudden illnesses caused by the breaking or blocking of a blood vessel in the brain), but it may increase the risk of having other types of strokes. And as you probably know, even moderate drinking and driving is a very risky combination. Driving a car requires the eyes, hands, and feet to work together to execute a complex series of tasks. With each drop of alcohol consumed, a person's ability to perform these tasks decreases.

Social Drinking

A person who drinks alcohol during special events, such as a formal dinner or party, is often called a social drinker. Social drinking may sound very much like moderate drinking, but it is somewhat different. Social drinkers usually pattern their drinking after that of other people around them. Depending on the occasion and the group one is with, this can mean anything from moderate drinking to alcohol abuse. We'll learn more about the roots of people's drinking habits in the next chapter.

Tolerance

If you've ever been around adults who drink, you may have noticed that some people don't seem to become affected by alcohol as much as others do. This is because everybody has a different level of tolerance to the drug. If people can drink without seeming intoxicated, they are said to "hold their liquor well." But this is not a good thing: researchers have learned that people who have high levels of tolerance may be drinking even more than those with lower levels. These drinkers may seem unaffected, but they still risk harming their health. Having a high tolerance may also make a person more likely to become an alcoholic.

Scientists and medical experts have reported that there are different types of tolerance to alcohol. Some have to do with the way alcohol is processed by a person's body; others relate to the social situations in which the person consumes the alcohol.

To measure the effects of alcohol on the body, experts measure a person's **blood alcohol concentration** (or **BAC**), the level of alcohol in the blood. How does this measure tolerance? Most adults can tolerate one drink consumed during a one-hour period (one drink is usually defined as 12 ounces of beer, 4.5 ounces of wine, or 1.5 ounces of 80-proof distilled spirits, meaning spirits with an alcohol content of 40 percent). Drinking at this rate produces little or no change in the average person's ability to function. That same drink ingested within five minutes, however, produces a high peak of BAC and therefore greater intoxication. Other factors that influence the effects of alcohol include the drinker's mood and body weight.

Longtime abusers of alcohol usually become "functionally tolerant." This means that the brain keeps functioning in spite of the problems that the drug creates. These drinkers may not appear intoxicated, but the amount of alcohol in their blood would make most people completely drunk or even kill them. People with functional tolerance can be dangerous because they may drink a great deal but still believe they are capable of driving, because they don't feel drunk. On the other hand, people with **acute** tolerance feel drunk soon after they begin to drink rather than later.

A group of college students drinking during spring break. Binge drinking—consuming five or more drinks in quick succession—is a major problem among underage drinkers. In 1997, 15 percent of eighth graders and 25 percent of tenth graders reported binge drinking. Among young people 12 to 17 years old, alcohol is the drug most often used—even though the legal drinking age in the United States is 21.

A different kind of tolerance occurs when a person frequently drinks in the same place or at the same time with the same people. This kind of tolerance can occur even in social drinkers. In one study, one group of social drinkers was given alcohol to drink in a room that looked like an office, while another group of social

Along with tobacco and marijuana, alcohol is a gateway drug: abusing it can lead to use of other drugs, such as cocaine and heroin, that are even more dangerous. The chart at right shows the results of a 1997 study by the National Household Survey on Drug Abuse. Almost 30 percent of

drinkers was given alcohol to drink in a room that looked like a bar. Then both groups were asked to take tests to measure hand and eye coordination. Most of the people who drank in the "bar" performed the test better than those in the "office." This study proved that the environment affects how the brain tolerates alcohol.

When a person is a **chronic** drinker, meaning that he or she drinks frequently or over a long period of time, the body begins using certain liver enzymes to

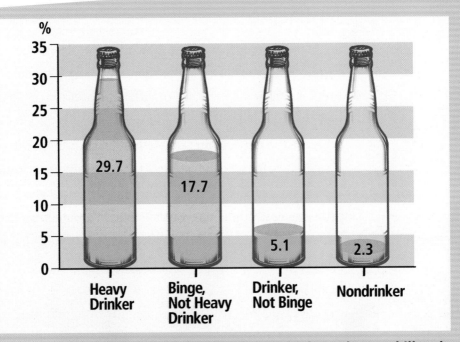

those who were defined as heavy drinkers also used illegal drugs in the month before the survey was taken. However, the number of nondrinkers who used drugs during the same period was only 2.3 percent—less than one-tenth the number of heavy drinkers who used illegal drugs.

break down the alcohol into other chemicals. These enzymes also break down certain types of medications, such as those taken to treat diabetes, prevent blood clotting, or calm the body. The chronic drinker who takes such medications may not feel their effects immediately, and he or she may overdose while trying to feel the full effect of the drug. The enzymes also break down pain relief medicines into substances that are poisonous to the liver, so chronic drinkers risk liver damage whenever they take painkillers.

Abstinence

Some people should not drink any alcohol at all. People who stay away from something that appeals to them, such as alcohol, are practicing **abstinence.** Pregnant women who drink even a small amount of alcohol increase the risk of causing birth defects in their babies. Research scientists have reported that pregnant monkeys given small doses of alcohol have babies who have problems with their nervous systems. Women who have two or three drinks a day during pregnancy have babies who are smaller than normal in weight, height, and head size.

Other people who should abstain from drinking are recovering alcoholics and people under the legal drinking age of 21. People who take certain medications or who have medical problems such as diabetes should also refrain from drinking. As we have seen, anyone who is planning to drive or perform some other skilled task should not drink.

A Nation of Drinkers

If alcohol is so dangerous, why is it so popular? The answer, unfortunately, is simple: we are a nation of alcohol drinkers. Seven out of every 10 American adults drink alcohol occasionally and one in 10 drinks it every day.

In 1993, historian W.J. Rorabaugh wrote a book about drinking in America called *The Alcoholic Republic: An American Tradition.* Rorabaugh says that Americans have always been among the heaviest drinkers in the world. "From colonial times to the present," he writes, "alcohol has been [everywhere] in American society, though the [drinking] of particular beverages and patterns of drinking in general have [changed]."

Men and women of many backgrounds and ethnic origins drink, although some groups generally have had histories of higher drinking levels than others. Throughout American history, some people have made attempts to stop others from drinking. These efforts have never worked for more than a short period, however. In Chapter 2, we will learn how people have struggled for thousands of years to enjoy the beneficial effects of alcohol without abusing it.

Alcohol is not a new drug. For thousands of years, people of various cultures have used it for medical, religious, and recreational purposes. This 16-century painting by Michelangelo Caravaggio shows Bacchus, the ancient god of wine, as a wild reveler—the original "party animal."

ALCOHOL THROUGHOUT HISTORY

A lcohol is the oldest **psychoactive** (mind- and behavior-altering) drug known to humanity. Scientists believe that the first alcoholic beverage was probably made by accident. When yeast is mixed with a sugary, mashed-up food, alcohol is created. Someone probably tasted a mix like this and it made them feel different. By the time people were using written language, they wrote stories about how ancestors had passed down the "gift" of alcohol.

Long ago, alcohol was used as medicine and in religious ceremonies. People thought that it had magical powers. In ancient Babylonia (where Israel, Syria, and Jordan are today), religious stories often concerned the use of wine. One ancient tale comes from Persia, the area of the Middle East that is now Iran and Iraq. In 1700 B.C., the Persian king, Jamshid, loved grapes. He stored them in large jars to keep them fresh. One day, he found that one jar of grapes had spoiled, and he had his servant label the jar as poison. A woman living in King Jamshid's household became so ill with a headache that she tried to kill herself by eating the poison grapes. But the grapes had undergone a process called **fermentation,** which turned them to wine. Rather than killing her, the fermented grapes cured her headache.

The woman talked King Jamshid into eating the grapes. He liked them so much that he soon began purposely fermenting grape juice into wine. He called it *zeher-e-hoosh,* which means "delightful poison."

Soon after people learned how to make alcohol, they discovered that drinking too much of it was not a wise choice. In the Jewish religion, there are many warnings about alcohol. For example, the book of Proverbs says, "Wine is a mocker, strong drink is raging; and whoever is deceived thereby is not wise."

Alcohol in Ancient Greece and Rome

In 700 B.C., the ancient Greeks thought that a small amount of wine was good for the brain. Greek men would gather for meetings where food and watered-down wine would be served. Then the men would talk about religion or politics.

The Greeks considered moderation very important. Centuries later, when the Romans conquered Greece, they adopted many ideas of the Greeks. But the Romans didn't copy the Greek habit of drinking in moderation. Instead, Roman gatherings resembled drunken parties.

In 186 B.C., in an effort to stop widespread drunkenness, the Roman government prohibited people from having such gatherings. The government also destroyed half of Rome's vineyards and prohibited farmers from planting new ones.

Alcohol in the Middle Ages

In the 13th century, two chemists from Switzerland named Arnaldus de Villanova and Raymond Lully published a paper about the health benefits of drinking alcohol. Villanova and Lully claimed that alcohol, which they called "the water of life," had helped them both live to the age of 70. (Back then, most people lived about 35 years.) Before long, alcohol was being used as a cure for colds, baldness, deafness, and liver problems. People also drank it to improve memory and to gain personal courage.

Alcohol in the New World

When Europeans began settling in the New World during the 1600s, they brought alcohol with them. They were used to drinking alcohol beginning at an early age because water from European rivers and lakes was often too polluted for drinking.

By the time the Revolutionary War broke out in 1775, the American colonists were growing grain and making their own whiskey (a drink made from fermented grains like rye, corn, or barley). Drinking habits differed in the North and the South. In the North, the Puritans of New England followed a very strict religion.

They drank alcohol in moderation and believed that being drunk in public was unacceptable. The Puritans believed that drunkenness was against God's laws.

Unlike most of the northern colonies, the southern colonies were not founded by religious groups such as the Puritans, and the rules governing drinking weren't as strict. A candidate who wanted to be elected to public office often helped his campaign by buying voters a drink on Election Day. In 1755, George Washington lost an election in the Virginia House of Burgesses because he wouldn't buy the voters alcohol.

Alcohol in the Early 1800s

As the American taste for alcohol grew, a doctor named Benjamin Rush began to study the effects of alcohol on health. Rush believed that alcoholism was a disease. He favored drinking in moderation and wrote that too much hard liquor (a term that describes strongly alcoholic drinks) would harm people's health. But few people paid attention to Rush's theories.

By the early 1800s, almost all Americans drank whiskey—and they drank a lot of it. Per person, they drank three times as much whiskey as Americans do today. Most adults drank about seven gallons of pure alcohol each year! Children were given whiskey as soon as they could drink from a glass.

Even though people in the 19th century generally didn't live as long as we do today, they still experienced many health and social problems caused by excessive drinking. Some clergy (church officials) preached

An 1891 French advertisement for champagne, a special type of white wine that is carbonated like soda. During the same time in the United States, alcohol consumption had reached such a high level that states began passing laws against its use. Nearly 30 years later, the U.S. Congress passed the Eighteenth Amendment, which banned alcohol almost entirely.

against drinking alcohol, declaring that it was created by the devil. By the 1830s, there was a strong effort to stop alcohol consumption altogether.

Between 1825 and 1840, almost half of the American population stopped drinking alcohol, but its abuse was still causing problems. By the early 1900s, many people were calling for a national ban on alcohol.

Prohibition

In 1919, the Eighteenth Amendment to the U.S. Constitution was ratified, making it illegal to manufacture, transport, or sell any beverage with more than a tiny percentage (0.5 percent) of alcohol in it. The period when this law was in force was called Prohibition.

Although some people did stop drinking during Prohibition, many others continued to drink as much as ever. Criminals imported or made alcohol, and people who wanted to drink went to illegal bars called speakeasies. In many cities criminals paid bribes to police officers to look the other way while the Prohibition laws were broken. By 1933, the Twenty-first Amendment to the Constitution was passed, overturning Prohibition.

The Birth of Alcoholics Anonymous

In 1935, a doctor in Akron, Ohio, named Bob Smith met a businessman from New York City named Bill Wilson. Both men were addicted to alcohol, but Wilson had found a way to get sober and stay that way. He told Smith about a program he was following that helped him overcome his problem. The program required honesty, responsibility for one's actions, and belief in a higher power. It also subscribed to the belief that you can help yourself by helping others. Together, Smith and Wilson founded an organization called Alcoholics Anonymous (AA), whose members abided by the principles Wilson had learned.

These people are attempting to break the powerful hold that alcohol addiction has on their lives by attending an Alcoholics Anonymous (AA) meeting. AA is a worldwide self-help group that offers support to people working to overcome their addiction.

Today, millions of alcoholics get help from a worldwide network of AA groups. Families of alcoholics learn how to deal with the problems caused by alcoholism in groups called Al-Anon. Teenagers and preteens can rely on a self-help network of groups called Alateen. All these groups use the same guidelines for getting and staying sober, a system called the Twelve Steps Program. We'll talk more about this program in Chapter 6.

A 22-year-old alcoholic living on the streets pleads for money from passersby. Despite what you may believe, even young people can fall victim to alcoholism or problem drinking. Alcohol abuse can damage the brain, liver, nervous system, and digestive system. Alcoholism has also been linked to heart, gland, and muscle diseases.

ALCOHOL'S EFFECTS ON THE BODY

When you eat food or drink beverages, your body begins to break down the substances as soon as they enter your mouth. This process is called digestion. Your body then uses the vitamins, minerals, and proteins from digested foods and beverages for nourishment and energy. The unusable remains or by-products are then eliminated. This entire process is called **metabolism.**

But alcohol is a very mild toxin, or poison. Just as it would with any other poison, your body tries to get rid of alcohol from the moment you drink it.

After it has been metabolized, very small amounts of alcohol leave the body when a drinker exhales or urinates. But the rest of the alcohol goes through the bloodstream to every organ, including the brain.

When alcohol enters the bloodstream, the body tries

to get rid of it through a process called oxidation. The body uses enzymes to break the alcohol down into non-toxic substances, like carbon dioxide and water, which are then removed from the bloodstream by the liver and kidneys. You exhale the carbon dioxide and eliminate the water by perspiring or urinating.

Male and Female Drinkers

Women's bodies have a harder time getting rid of alcohol than do men's. For one thing, women have almost no ADH in the lining of their stomachs, so more alcohol goes directly into their small intestines. That means that even if a woman drinks the same amount as a man, she may absorb more alcohol and will have a higher blood alcohol level than the man.

Women also have a higher percentage of fat and less water in their bodies than men do. Alcohol dissolves in water but not in fat, so it doesn't dissolve into women's body tissues as quickly as it does into men's. As a result, alcohol is not metabolized in women's bodies as quickly as it is in men's bodies.

Blood Alcohol Concentration

When a person is arrested for drunk driving, the police check that driver's BAC, a scientific measurement of how intoxicated the driver is. This test, called a Breathalyzer test, measures the level of alcohol that has been absorbed but not metabolized by the person's body. This small proportion—usually about five percent of the total amount of alcohol consumed—can tell a police

A man in a Colorado bar blows into a straw to measure his blood alcohol concentration (BAC). His breath is analyzed by a computer, which estimates his BAC so that the man can tell whether he can safely get behind the wheel of a car. In most states, it is illegal to drive with a BAC of more than .10 percent. However, with the first drink one takes, the ability to drive and perform other tasks that involve coordination starts to decline.

officer how much alcohol is in the driver's blood. It takes a very small amount of alcohol to be over the legal limit permitted to operate a car or other vehicle.

After a person has one drink, it takes 30 to 45 minutes for the body to get rid of the alcohol. While the person is drinking the alcohol, his or her body is working hard to get rid of it. Drinking alcohol is sometimes called a "chemical insult" to the body because it can be very damaging to the body's organs and tissues. A famous writer named Truman Capote called his own alcoholism "a severe insult to the brain." Scientific research tells us that alcohol does, in fact, damage the brain. In some cases, the damage is permanent.

Alcohol and the Brain

The brain has many ways of processing information, and alcohol impairs nearly every one of them. For example, your brain controls the way your eyes move and the way they work in combination with your hands. Alcohol makes it difficult for the brain to coordinate complex tasks.

Steering a car is a complicated job for the brain. Ideally, the brain makes the hands react quickly to what the eyes see. At the same time, the eyes must also focus very quickly on many different things and keep track of them as they move. Even low and moderate BAC levels lessen the brain's ability to control these tasks.

But alcohol does still more to make driving a car difficult. A driver who has any amount of alcohol in his or her bloodstream needs more time than a nondrinker to read a street sign or traffic signal.

One of the basic requirements of safe driving is that the brain be able to do many things at once. Drivers must be able to know where other cars and people are, read traffic signals, and keep the car in the proper lane while going in the proper direction at an appropriate speed.

But under the influence of alcohol, the brain can't do all of those jobs equally well. Alcohol makes the brain pay too much attention to one job and not enough attention to others. So the driver might be able to read all the traffic signs but not be able to steer the car in a straight line at the same time.

Brain Damage

Many alcoholics suffer brain damage from drinking too much. When scientists tested people who were in treatment for alcoholism, they found that out of every 10 people, 4 to 7 had lost some ability to solve problems, to think in more complicated ways, and to recall things they were asked to remember.

Researchers report that the brain of an alcoholic can be physically changed by alcohol. Alcohol restricts blood flow, so the brain receives less nourishment and oxygen than it needs to function properly. Some brains of alcoholics show reduced electrical activity. This means that, compared with a normal brain, the alcoholic brain is sending fewer signals to, and receiving fewer from, the rest of the body.

In very severe cases of alcoholism, brain damage continues even after the person stops drinking. Some of the damage comes directly from the alcohol, but the alcoholic's poor eating habits or physical injuries suffered while drinking also contribute to the damage.

Some researchers say that alcohol has the same effect on the brain's thought processes as aging does. So, just as an elderly person may have problems remembering, an alcoholic may experience memory lapses or become forgetful.

Researchers say that some of the brain damage that alcohol causes is reversible if the drinker stops drinking. This may simply be because the person is no longer causing continued damage by drinking alcohol. Most likely, he or she is also eating a more balanced daily diet and has resumed a healthier way of relating to family members and coworkers. Some research shows that people who engage in mental exercises and other activities that encourage the brain to work can restore much of their mental function.

The Liver

The liver is the largest organ in the body, and it is even more vulnerable than the brain to alcohol's effects. Liver disease caused by alcoholism is a serious ailment. In the United States, alcohol is the most common cause of illness and death from liver problems.

The liver plays an important role in keeping the body healthy. It filters the blood to remove toxins. It also secretes bile into the small intestine to digest food and absorb fats, and it works with other systems in the body to metabolize foods and liquids.

The liver also regulates blood clotting and blood fluidity. It changes metabolized protein into urea so that the kidneys can eliminate it. The liver stores vitamins, breaks down cholesterol, metabolizes and stores sugar, and turns amino acids into proteins. A person must have a healthy liver to survive.

Gross! This photograph shows three human livers. The most important job of the liver is to keep the body free of toxins—such as alcohol—by filtering the blood. Heavy drinking can cause a normal liver (left) to become fatty (center), or develop a very serious disease called cirrhosis (right), in which scar tissue replaces healthy cells.

Alcohol-Related Liver Problems

Alcohol can cause any of three problems in the liver. The first is a condition called fatty liver, which occurs because alcohol interferes with the liver's ability to metabolize fat. The excess fat in the liver dissipates after the drinker stops using alcohol. Fatty liver does not cause symptoms of illness.

The second alcohol-related liver problem, alcoholic **hepatitis,** is a serious inflammation of the liver that sometimes strikes heavy drinkers. The symptoms are fever, abdominal pain, and jaundice. Alcoholic hepatitis can be fatal.

The third and worst alcoholic liver condition is called **cirrhosis.** No one knows exactly how alcohol causes cirrhosis, but the disease, which often develops with little warning, destroys healthy cells in the liver and replaces them with scar tissue. The scar tissue closes off blood vessels and eventually prevents the liver from working. Liver transplants sometimes save people who are at risk of dying from alcoholic cirrhosis.

An alcoholic may have all three of these liver conditions at the same time. The person can recover from fatty liver and alcoholic hepatitis if he or she stops drinking. Occasionally, this can also halt the progression of cirrhosis, but usually the disease steadily worsens until it proves fatal.

Liver disease caused by alcoholism can also make the veins in a person's throat bleed, make his or her kidneys stop working, cause fluid to collect in the stomach, and even cause brain damage.

Eating

Excessive alcohol consumption can not only cause serious organ damage, but it can also affect the way the body digests and uses food. Most alcoholics don't eat well, and many receive up to half of their daily calories from alcohol. Even if an alcoholic does eat well, however, alcohol affects the digestive system, impairing the body's ability to draw and store nutrients from food.

By now, you may be wondering why people want to drink alcohol in the first place if it can be so harmful. One simple answer is that low to moderate doses of alcohol can make a person feel good. Chapter 4 explores the ways this good feeling can lead to the disease of alcoholism.

Some people use alcohol to escape stress or frustration. Others drink to relieve pain or anger. In reality, alcohol abuse, like other kinds of drug abuse, does not solve problems. In fact, it usually creates even greater ones.

WHY DO PEOPLE USE ALCOHOL?

I f alcohol is so harmful, why are adults allowed to drink it? More important, why would they want to? As you learned from Chapter 1, about 1 in every 10 people drink alcohol daily. Seven in 10 drink alcohol at least once in a while. Why?

Habit

Alcohol has been a part of human history for thousands of years. People from around the world have used it in religious ceremonies, as medicine, and in celebrations. People from a variety of different cultural backgrounds make up the United States and form its national attitudes about drinking. Although not everyone agrees, most people value the legal right to drink alcohol.

Advertising

The companies that make and sell alcoholic beverages advertise their products on TV and radio, in newspapers and magazines, and on billboards. The pictures show beautiful women and handsome men having fun and relaxing with friends. These advertisements tell viewers that if they want to have fun and be seen as handsome or pretty, they should drink alcohol. The advertisers want to send the message that alcohol is more than just a drink; it is a reward that people give to themselves and their friends.

Getting a "Buzz"

Some people say they drink simply because they like the taste of beer, wine, or liquor. But you can buy alcohol-free beer. And sparkling grape juice looks, smells, and tastes very similar to wine. Why don't more people who drink because they like the taste just buy beverages without alcohol in them?

The truth is, a small amount of alcohol can make a person feel relaxed and friendly. Alcohol brings on a feeling called **euphoria,** which is a sense of happiness or well-being. Some people call this feeling a "buzz" or a "high." People sometimes seek to bring on the feeling by drinking alcohol.

Drinking to feel good, however, can lead to danger. A person might drink one, two, or a dozen drinks in one sitting. Unfortunately, making the decision to stop drinking or to avoid becoming intoxicated becomes

You may think the "Budweiser frogs" commercials are amusing, but a number of anti-drug groups, including Mothers Against Drunk Driving (MADD), do not. They believe that advertisements with kid-friendly characters—such as these frogs or the "Joe Camel" figure in cigarette ads—target kids who are too young to use these drugs legally. What do you think? Do these kinds of ads make using drugs look like fun?

more difficult with each additional drink a person consumes. When the body receives more alcohol than it can metabolize, it reacts unfavorably to the alcohol overload. This reaction is called intoxication.

Intoxication

What does being intoxicated feel like? Heavy drinkers may experience euphoria but they also feel woozy or sleepy. If they are extremely drunk, their vision becomes blurry and they feel nauseated. They may throw up or pass out. Drinking more than the body can metabolize or get rid of can be fatal.

Drinking would be much less risky if everyone could control the amount they drink. But a person is not a chemistry set: one doesn't react to the same amount of alcohol in the same, predictable way every time one drinks. And no two people react to alcohol in the same way.

When a person drinks alcohol while eating, the food absorbs some of the alcohol, so the person feels less intoxicated. On the other hand, if someone drinks on an empty stomach, the alcohol has an even more powerful effect.

Also, responsible drinkers don't drink quickly. They sip one drink slowly over a long period of time. Because the body begins getting rid of the alcohol immediately, less alcohol is in the person's body at any one time, and the person runs a lower risk of becoming intoxicated.

Some people, however, are chronic (long-term) heavy drinkers. Their bodies have adjusted to the presence of large amounts of alcohol. If a nondrinker were to suddenly drink the same amount as a chronic drinker, the nondrinker might actually die of alcohol poisoning.

Using Alcohol as an Escape

Some people use alcohol-induced euphoria to get away from the pain in their lives. As strange as it may sound, the attractive actress Drew Barrymore became an alcoholic in part because she felt ugly, stupid, and lonely. If a famous movie star might use alcohol to deal with feelings of unworthiness, it's not surprising that many ordinary people use it to dull their negative feelings as well. A person who drinks to escape bad feelings often wants to drink more and more to keep those feelings away because the body begins to develop a physical tolerance for alcohol. The person then has to drink more than before to produce the same effect.

When drinkers become addicted to alcohol, they don't feel like themselves unless they have alcohol in their system. If an alcoholic wakes up in the morning after drinking, he or she may still need another drink to feel "normal" again.

The Disease of Alcoholism

Some adults are able to drink responsibly. They drink in moderation and they don't do dangerous things such as driving a car or a boat after drinking.

Other adults cannot control their drinking. They drink even though it hurts their families and friends. They lose their jobs because of drinking. They kill or injure themselves or other people because they drive while intoxicated.

The idea that alcoholism is a disease is not a new one. In 200 B.C., a Roman judge named Domitius Elpinus suggested that uncontrolled drinking might be a disease. But until the middle of the 20th century, most doctors thought alcoholism was a weakness of character and that alcoholics were bad or immoral people who couldn't control their behavior.

Mark S. Gold, M.D., author of *The Good News About Drugs and Alcohol,* says that when people realized that

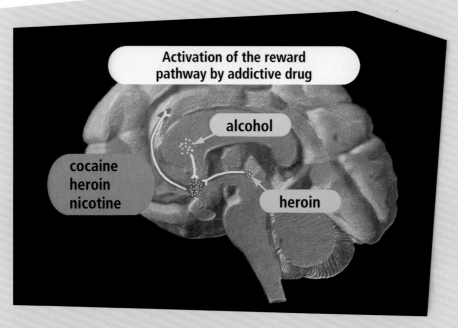

Activation of the reward
pathway by addictive drug

cocaine
heroin
nicotine

alcohol

heroin

**Drug addiction is a disease of the brain: although people can
choose to take drugs, they do not choose to become addicted.
This illustration shows how drugs such as alcohol cause addiction
by activating an area in the brain called the "reward pathway."
Behaviors that are necessary to survival—eating, drinking,
procreating, and nurturing—create pleasurable feelings in the brain
to "reward" humans and insure that they repeat them. Addictive
drugs activate this pathway also, so that the addicted person
continues to use the drug despite severe negative consequences.**

addiction was a disease, they made one of the most
important medical discoveries of the 20th century. "It
has helped millions of people to stop blaming themselves
for their illness," says Gold.

Donald W. Goodwin, M.D., has written a book called
Alcoholism: The Facts. He explains that some people still
reject the idea that alcoholism is a disease:

One reason people, including doctors, have trouble viewing alcoholism as a disease like cancer is that alcoholism is associated with having fun and fun is not usually associated with disease.

Why or how a person "catches" a disease is not important. . . . Why alcoholics drink is not important to the diagnosis of alcoholism.

A New Category of Disease

Enoch Gordis, M.D., the director of the NIAAA, thinks that alcoholism and other addictions are a new category of disease. "How can we say that alcoholism is a disease when most treatment is talking and the patient recovers by using willpower?" he asked. "The answer is not that alcoholism is a sin or character defect, but that we are dealing with a new category of disease."

Gordis explains that throughout medical history, the idea of what disease is has changed. At one time, people thought some diseases, such as epilepsy, were caused by the devil living in a person's body. In the case of addictions such as alcoholism, the definition of disease also has to be changed. When a person is an alcoholic, says Gordis, the reward circuits in the brain tell the person to seek alcohol. Normally, the reward circuits tell us to do things that help us live, such as eating, sleeping, and finding shelter. But addictions create drives that tell the brain to do certain things to the exclusion of all else, even the body's well-being. And those messages become stronger than the memory of how bad it feels to be drunk.

Another confusing part of alcoholism is that the

disease's pattern changes throughout a person's life. "There are periods lasting days, weeks, or years when the alcoholic doesn't drink at all, even without formal treatment," Gordis says. "There are times when even if he starts drinking, he doesn't go on a bender. Until we know more about these variations . . . the condition called alcoholism appears to be random."

Choice

Does this mean that an alcoholic has no choice but to drink? After all, no one takes a first drink of alcohol with the intent to destroy his or her life and the lives of family members.

It is important to distinguish between the disease of alcoholism and the alcoholic person. Just as someone suffering from diabetes is not responsible for developing the disease, an alcoholic cannot be blamed for his or her addiction. However, that person *is* responsible for getting treatment for the disease and for his or her behavior once the disease is diagnosed. For example, let's say a man who is diagnosed with diabetes decides not to take the medication prescribed by his doctor. While driving home from work one day, he goes into shock, a condition that occurs when too much insulin is in a diabetic's system. The man slips into a coma and causes an accident.

Is the man responsible for the accident? Yes, but not because he is diabetic. He is responsible because he knew about his disease but chose to ignore medical advice on how to keep himself healthy. In the same way, alcoholics who know about their condition yet choose not to take steps to control it are responsible for the consequences of their actions.

People who have alcoholism in their families should be especially careful to avoid alcohol. "A child of an alcoholic parent is at high risk," says Gordis. "Young people who are less sensitive than their friends to the effects of alcohol are likely to increase their drinking and are at greatly increased risk for alcoholism as adults."

Children of Alcoholics

There are 6.6 million kids under age 18 who live in a house with at least one alcoholic parent. If you are the son or daughter of an alcoholic, you have been robbed of what should be a joyous time in your life. Kids should be free to concentrate on friends, school, and growing up. But in homes where one or both parents are alcoholic, the kids take on the job of being the adults.

Kids from alcoholic families often say they are depressed, anxious, and filled with stress. Sometimes kids with alcoholic parents act out their pain by fighting, skipping school, stealing, or lying.

Many schools have guidance counselors who are specially trained to help kids deal with the pain of having an alcoholic parent. If you have a parent with a drinking problem, talk to a teacher or guidance counselor and get some help. You don't have to struggle with this problem alone.

Sometimes, however, the problem drinker in the family is a young person. We'll discuss the special dangers of underage drinking in Chapter 5.

According to government statistics, nearly 20 percent of teens from ages 12 to 17 drink alcohol. Think alcohol can't hurt you? Before you decide to try a beer or wine cooler, read this chapter. What you learn may change your mind.

UNDERAGE DRINKING

E ven though it is illegal for people under 21 years old to drink, underage drinking is a serious problem in the United States. Alcohol is the most widely used and abused drug among young people. About two out of every three teenagers who drink say they can buy alcoholic beverages from stores or bars without any help from an adult.

If many adults can drink alcohol responsibly, why is it so bad for kids to drink?

Alcohol's Effects on Growth and Puberty

When scientists studied alcohol's effects on young rats, they found that high doses delayed puberty in both the male and female animal. Young rats who were given large amounts of alcohol also had slower bone growth and weaker bones than the rats that were not fed alcohol.

No one knows if the same effect is true for young people because scientists don't do alcohol experiments on children. However, there is more than enough scientific evidence to show that alcohol has a variety of harmful effects on the human body at any age. This is reason enough for young people to abstain from drinking.

There is also a big difference between the reasons adults and teenagers give for drinking alcohol. Richard Heyman, chairman of the American Academy of Pediatrics Committee on Substance Abuse, says that adults *who drink responsibly* do so because they are thirsty or want to feel good. "But kids who drink beer don't drink it to quench their thirst or to feel good," he says. "They drink it to get smashed. Unlike most adults, kids drink to get drunk."

Binge Drinking

About 11 million Americans from ages 12 to 20 drink at least one alcoholic beverage a month. Of that group, 4.8 million are what experts call binge drinkers. A binge drinker drinks five or more drinks in one sitting. This behavior often begins during the early teens, and is most common among people ages 18 to 22.

In a 1994 survey, 28 percent of high school seniors, 41 percent of 21- and 22-year-olds, and 25 percent of 31- and 32-year-olds said they were binge drinkers.

Underage Drinking and Social Skills

Developing social skills is often a difficult, complicated process. Feeling good about yourself while trying to make friends and do well in school or sports takes a lot self-confidence.

Most kids experience at least occasional feelings of awkwardness, pain, or anger. Drinking makes those feelings go away—at least for a while. But when a person uses alcohol to numb negative feelings, drinking becomes a substitute for learning how to deal with these

Unfortunately, some teens turn to alcohol or other drugs in the mistaken belief that these substances will ease feelings of pain or frustration, make them feel more comfortable in social situations, or allow them to fit in with others.

Studies have found a direct link between cigarette smoking and alcohol abuse. A 1997 survey found that the rate of heavy alcohol use among current smokers is nearly five times that of nonsmokers.

emotions. If a young person continues to drink and becomes dependent on alcohol, the addiction just adds to his or her social problems.

Using alcohol to get away from stress actually creates more problems for young people because of the way alcohol reacts in the body. Alcohol is a central nervous system depressant (a substance that slows down or reduces a bodily function). Although the first drink may make a person feel better or more relaxed, the longer that person drinks, the worse he or she feels. Alcohol provides only temporary relief and does little to get rid of the drinker's problems. In other words, even if drinking makes you feel better for the time being, you're almost certain to feel worse in the end.

Early Drinking

The use of alcohol or any drug at an early age may indicate that the person might develop alcohol and drug problems in the future. A study of 43,000 young people conducted by the NIAAA found that the younger a person is when he or she starts to drink, the greater the chance that the person will have a drinking problem as an adult. For example, 40 percent of people who began drinking before the age of 15 eventually became addicted to alcohol. Only 10 percent of people who waited until they were 21 to begin drinking became addicted.

U.S. Secretary for Health and Human Services Donna E. Shalala has observed that the NIAAA study shows just how harmful it is for young people to drink. "Parents, schools, and communities need to say to our young people with one voice that underage drinking can jeopardize health and lifetime prospects," she says.

Even though underage drinking is illegal, junior-high, middle, and senior-high school students drink 1.1 billion cans of beer a year and consume 35 percent of all wine coolers sold in the United States. A 1997 survey by the Department of Health and Human Services showed that more than 20 percent of kids ages 12 to 17 currently drink alcohol.

Peer Pressure and Advertising

The *Weekly Reader* National Survey on Drugs and Alcohol reports that 3 out of every 10 kids in the fourth to sixth grades feel a lot of pressure from their

Although young people are less likely to drive than adults, their accident rates are substantially higher than those of adult drivers. In fact, youth is cited as one of the most significant factors in auto accidents. Half of all car accidents—the leading cause of death among teenagers—involve alcohol. And in 1996, a study called Drug Use Forecasting, which reports on drug-related arrests, found that more than 11,000 American teens under 18 years old were arrested for violating DWI (driving while intoxicated) laws.

classmates to drink beer. In the same survey, more than half the students from grades 5 to 12 report that alcohol advertisements encouraged them to drink. The National Council on Alcoholism and Drug Dependence (NCADD) estimates that youth in the United States see alcohol consumed on TV, in movies, and in real life an average of 75,000 times before they reach the legal drinking age.

Why Some Kids Drink

Richard Heyman of the American Academy of Pediatrics Committee on Substance Abuse, says teenagers drink for many reasons.

"Some kids start because they are a little rebellious," he says. "Others start because they are offered alcoholic beverages by a friend or adult. And some drink because it is portrayed as absolutely normal by the media, by advertising agencies, and by the sports industry."

Kids who are abused or depressed may use alcohol and drugs to feel good. Other kids use alcohol because they have what Heyman calls an image gap. "The bigger the gap between how a teenager sees himself and how he wishes he looks, acts or seems, the more likely he is to need something to fill that gap," he says. "A lot of kids choose alcohol and drugs to do that."

Windle also reports that the highest percentage of teenagers who drink alcohol are Caucasians (whites) and Native Americans. The next-highest percentage of alcohol users are Hispanic teens. The groups of teenagers who drink the least, according to statistics, are African Americans and Asian Americans.

"There is some evidence that the parents of African-American children more frequently speak to their children about alcohol and substance abuse than Caucasian parents and establish clear rules for drug use, including consequences for breaking the rules," Windle states.

Drinking and Driving

Car accidents are the single greatest cause of death for teenagers. In 1994, nearly 7,800 drivers ages 16 to 20 were involved in car accidents in which people died. Although none of those drivers was old enough to drink legally, 23 percent of them had in fact been drinking alcohol before the crash.

Good News

There are some indications that young people are getting the message about the dangers of alcohol. Mothers Against Drunk Driving (MADD) reports a trend toward fewer intoxicated young drivers in fatal car crashes. From 1983 to 1994, the number of young drunk drivers involved in accidents went down 14 percent. This was the largest drop for any age group during that time.

The campaign against underage drinking isn't just for adults. A group called Students Against Driving Drunk (SADD) is a national organization founded in 1981 by Bob Anastas, a Massachusetts hockey coach, who saw two of his star players die in alcohol-related accidents within one week. SAAD is led by high school students who focus on reducing the number of alcohol-related

These shoes represent the 724 people killed in alcohol-related auto accidents in Florida during 1995. The display was set up in the state capital of Tallahassee by Mothers Against Drunk Driving (MADD), which is active in making legislators aware of the dangers of drunk driving. Since MADD was founded in the early 1980s, the number of young drivers involved in alcohol-related accidents has dropped by 14 percent.

driving accidents and helping kids and young adults resist peer pressure to drink. One of the ways SADD members do this is by urging kids to call their parents for transportation rather than ride with someone who has been drinking. SADD stresses that it condemns alcohol and substance abuse but not the abusers themselves.

Former major league baseball star Dave Winfield discusses the negatives of underage alcohol use with kids in a Los Angeles program called Ready or Not: Talking with Kids About Alcohol. Ready or Not also teaches parents and other adults how to talk to children about the dangers of alcohol use. Does your community have antidrug programs such as this one? Check the yellow pages of your phone book or go to your local library to find out.

WHERE DO YOU GO FROM HERE?

The best way to avoid all the legal, safety, and health problems of alcohol is not to drink. But how do you say no to alcohol when friends offer it to you?

Instead of waiting until this happens, plan ahead. Imagine yourself in the situation. You don't need to make excuses: just say no and keep it simple and direct. Your courage may give other kids around you the strength to say no, too. But even if you are the only one who refuses to drink, saying no is still the right choice.

Don't put yourself in a dangerous situation. If you know that there will be alcohol at a party or sleepover, make other plans. If you know that someone is planning to drink while driving, find another ride.

Seek alcohol-free activities. Join a team, learn a new hobby, or find a cause you believe in and work for it. Stay away from kids who drink or brag about getting drunk.

When Someone You Care About May Have a Drinking Problem

If you think someone you know may have a problem with alcohol, look for these warning signs:

- Does the person seem confused, feel tired a lot, or have trouble sleeping or eating?
- Does the person avoid family members? Does he or she frequently act angry or uncooperative? Does he or she seem very sad, or have rapid mood swings? Is the person becoming irresponsible or irritable?
- Has he or she changed friends? Did the person's grades drop? Is he or she frequently absent from or late for school?

Of course, some of these warning signs could also arise from other problems. A disturbance in eating and sleeping patterns, for example, may be the result of family problems or school anxiety. Extreme fatigue may be a sign of a physical or mental problem other than alcoholism.

To help someone with a possible alcohol problem, the Center for Substance Abuse Prevention offers these tips:

- Try to remain calm, unemotional, and honest in talking to your friend or loved one about his or her behavior and its results.
- Let the person with the problem know that you are learning about alcohol abuse and you are going to a support group.

Do You Have an Alcohol Problem?

Alcoholics Anonymous has developed the following set of questions to help teens learn whether they are abusing alcohol. Try to answer these questions honestly.

○ Do you drink because you have problems or to relax?

○ Do you drink when you get angry with other people such as your friends or parents?

○ Do you prefer to drink alone rather than with others?

○ Are your grades starting to slip? Are you goofing off with your responsibilities?

○ Have you ever tried to stop drinking or to drink less—and failed?

○ Have you begun drinking in the morning before school?

○ Do you gulp your drinks?

○ Do you ever have loss of memory from drinking?

○ Do you lie about your drinking?

○ Do you ever get into trouble when you're drinking?

○ Do you get drunk when you drink, even when you don't mean to?

○ Do you think it's cool to be able to hold your liquor?

If you can answer yes to any of these questions, you may have an alcohol problem. But take heart—you're not alone. Look at pages 75 to 77 in this book for suggestions on where to get help.

- Talk to someone you trust—a friend, a social worker, a clergy member, or someone who has had experience with treating alcohol abuse.
- Refuse to ride in a car or boat or on a motorcycle with anyone who has been drinking alcohol.

Be careful not to preach at the person or bribe him or her to quit drinking. Never argue with a person while he or she is drinking or drunk. Don't try to drink along with the problem drinker, or hide or pour out bottles of alcohol to keep the person from using it. Above all, remember that you are not responsible for the drinker's behavior. Try not to feel guilty about the way the person acts—it is not your fault, and it is not in your control.

Withdrawal

When someone quits after a prolonged period of continual drinking, the body can react with withdrawal symptoms such as shaking, seizures, and **hallucinations** (seeing or hearing things in a distorted way, or perceiving things that aren't real). Nowadays, doctors prescribe drugs to help control withdrawal symptoms and to keep the patient from suffering permanent physical effects, such as brain damage.

Relapsing

Some people go through treatment to stop drinking, but then begin drinking again. This is called a **relapse.** One expert says that about 90 percent of alcoholics experience at least one relapse within the first four years of becoming sober. The more severe an alcoholic's dependence, the more likely he or she will relapse. Also, alcoholism can permanently damage a person's ability to control his or her actions, so it may be harder for some alcoholics to resist relapsing. Recovering alcoholics also experience cravings—powerful urges to start drinking again. Craving reminds the drinker of both the euphoria of alcohol and the misery of having to go through withdrawal again.

Treatment

The most popular form of alcoholism treatment in the United States is provided by AA, the organization described in Chapter 2. AA treatment is built on what is called the Twelve Steps Program. The most important part of the program is having members admit that alcohol has ruined their lives and that they are responsible for stopping their alcohol consumption. Although AA is not a religious organization, members also acknowledge that a "higher power"—a positive force greater than themselves—can help them recover. AA members must also try to make amends for any wrong or harm they may have done to others while under the influence of alcohol.

People in AA do not go through recovery alone. One of the principles of the organization is that members help one another by sharing their experiences in regular meetings. Usually, longtime members also "sponsor" newer members by agreeing to be available outside meetings should they need help.

Since the founding of AA, millions of alcoholics have used the Twelve Steps Program to win back their sobriety (the state of being sober). The families of alcoholics have also established a support group, known as Al-Anon. Today Al-Anon has 600,000 members in 112 countries.

In the mid-1950s, the teenage son of AA and Al-Anon parents started Alateen for teenagers. Alateen has 4,000 local groups and has expanded to include pre-teen family members.

Other Treatments

Doctors prescribe several kinds of drugs to combat the symptoms of alcoholism and withdrawal. Minor tranquilizers such as Valium can slow or stop the shaking. Antidepressants can help treat the depression that often accompanies alcohol recovery. Unfortunately, no medicine can stop alcoholics from using alcohol again.

Antabuse is a drug that helps alcoholics avoid drinking. It does not reduce physical cravings for alcohol. Instead, when taken daily, it makes users feel extremely sick if they also drink alcohol. Knowing that this can happen, recovering alcoholics on Antabuse avoid drinking and thus gain some control over their cravings.

Psychotherapy is an important part of many alcohol treatment programs. In psychotherapy, a licensed mental health professional helps people solve their problems through talk. People in "rehab" (drug and alcohol rehabilitation clinics) often get both individual and group psychotherapy.

High school students all over the country have driven this "Drunk Driving Simulator" around a course. The car has a special computer that adjusts the steering and braking controls to mimic how a person's reactions are slowed when under the influence of alcohol. Educational programs like this one allow teens to be better informed when making decisions about drinking and driving.

Preventing Alcoholism

The only way to guarantee that you will never become an alcoholic is not to drink alcohol. Even after you gain the legal right to drink, you will always have the right to *choose* not to drink. And if you do decide to drink, you will also always have the right to choose *how much* you will drink. Make the right choice for you, and the future will be yours to enjoy.

GLOSSARY

abstinence—staying away from a food or drink that appeals to one.

acute—very sharp or intense, or happening suddenly and lasting only for a short time.

addiction—a condition of some drug users that is caused by repeated drug use. An addicted user becomes physically dependent on the drug and continues to take it, despite severe negative consequences.

alcohol abuse—a pattern of drinking that makes a person unable to perform normal tasks. The alcohol abuser may drink while driving or doing other tasks requiring increased coordination, may be arrested for disorderly conduct or may hurt someone while intoxicated, and continue to drink even though doing so harms family relationships and friendships.

alcohol dehydrogenase (ADH)—an enzyme in the lining of the stomach that helps to break down alcohol.

alcoholism—a disease characterized by excessive and often compulsive consumption of alcoholic beverages.

blood alcohol concentration (BAC)—a measurement of the amount of alcohol in the bloodstream.

chronic—occurring over a long period of time or recurring frequently.

cirrhosis—a chronic, alcohol-induced disease of the liver that destroys liver cells and creates scar tissue that blocks circulation. Cirrhosis eventually causes liver failure and death.

craving—great desire or longing, especially an abnormally strong need for drugs or alcohol.

enzyme—a protein found in living organisms that aids a chemical reaction in the body, such as digestion.

euphoria—an intense feeling of happiness or well-being.

fermentation—a chemical process by which the sugar in liquid turns into alcohol and a gas. Yeast or certain bacteria can cause fermentation in fruit juices.

hallucination—a vision or sound that isn't real, or a distorted perception of objects or events.

hepatitis—a disease or condition marked by inflammation of the liver.

intoxication—the condition of being drunk.

metabolism—the process by which living things change food into energy and living tissue and then dispose of waste material.

minor tranquilizer—a drug used to reduce anxiety, tension, or other mental disturbances. Minor tranquilizers may also be prescribed to relieve the symptoms of alcohol withdrawal.

moderation—avoidance of excessive alcohol consumption.

physical dependence—addiction; a state in which a drug user's body has adapted to require regular doses of the drug to function normally. Stopping the drug causes withdrawal symptoms.

psychoactive—affecting the mind or behavior.

relapse—to fall back into a former, worse state.

stroke—a sudden illness caused by the breaking or blocking of a blood vessel in the brain. Strokes can cause coma, paralysis on one side of the body, and loss of speech; they may also be fatal.

tolerance—a condition in which a drug user requires increasing amounts of a drug to achieve the same level of intoxication once obtained from using smaller amounts.

withdrawal—a process that occurs when a person who is physically dependent on a drug stops taking the drug.

BIBLIOGRAPHY

Center for Substance Abuse Prevention (CSAP). "Tips for Teens About Alcohol." National Clearinghouse for Alcohol and Drug Information (NCADI) Publication No. PHD323. Rockville, MD: CSAP, 1996.

Goodwin, Donald W. *Alcoholism: the Facts.* New York: Oxford University Press, 1997.

Lang, Alan R. *Alcohol: Teenage Drinking.* New York: Chelsea House Publishers, 1992.

Monroe, Judy. *Alcohol.* Springfield, NJ: Enslow Publishers, 1994.

Mothers Against Drunk Driving (MADD). "Some Myths About Alcohol." http://www.madd.org/UNDER21/ youth_myths.shtml. Irving, TX: MADD, 1998.

———. "The Unbelievable Truth About Being a Teenage Boy." http://www.madd.org/UNDER21/youth_guys.shtml. Irving, TX: MADD, 1998.

———. "The Unbelievable Truth About Being a Teenage Girl." http://www.madd.org/UNDER21/youth_girls.shtml. Irving, TX: MADD, 1998.

NCADI. *A Guide for Teens: Does Your Friend Have an Alcohol or Other Drug Problem? What You Can Do to Help.* NCADI Publication No. PHD688. Rockville, MD: NCADI, 1994.

Peacock, Nancy. *Drowning Our Sorrows: Psychological Effects of Alcohol Abuse.* Philadelphia: Chelsea House Publishers, 1999.

FIND OUT MORE ABOUT ALCOHOL AND OTHER DRUG ABUSE

The following list includes agencies, organizations, and websites that provide information about alcohol and other drugs. You can also find out where to go for help with an alcohol or other drug problem.

Many national organizations have local chapters listed in your phone directory. Look under "Drug Abuse and Addiction" or "Alcoholism" to find resources in your area.

Agencies and Organizations in the United States

Al-Anon Family Group Headquarters
1600 Corporate Landing Parkway
Virginia Beach, VA 23454-5617
http://www.al-anon.alateen.org
757-563-1600
800-344-2666 (United States)
800-443-4525 (Canada)

Alcoholics Anonymous (AA) World Services
475 Riverside Drive, 11th Floor
New York, NY 10115
212-870-3400
http://www.alcoholics-anonymous.org

American Council for Drug Education
164 West 74th Street
New York, NY 10023
212-758-8060 or 800-488-DRUG (3784)
http://www.acde.org/
wlittlefield@phoenixhouse.org

American Society of Addiction Medicine
4601 North Park Avenue, Arcade Suite 101
Chevy Chase, MD 20815
301-656-3920
http://www.asam.org

Center for Substance Abuse Treatment
Information and Treatment Referral Hotline
11426-28 Rockville Pike
Suite 410
Rockville, MD 20852
800-662-HELP (4357)

Children of Alcoholics Foundation, Inc.
555 Madison Avenue
4th Floor
New York, NY 10022
212-754-0656
800-359-COAF (2623)

Mothers Against Drunk Driving (MADD)
P.O. Box 541688
Dallas, TX 75354-1688
800-GET-MADD (438-6233)
http://www.madd.org
info@madd.org

National Clearinghouse for Alcohol and Drug Information (NCADI)
P.O. Box 2345
Rockville, MD 20847-2345
800-729-6686
800-487-4889 TDD
800-HI-WALLY (449-2559, Children's Line)
http://www.health.org/

National Council on Alcoholism and Drug Dependence (NCADD)
12 West 21st Street
New York, NY 10010
800-NCA-CALL (622-2255)
http://www.ncadd.org

National Institute on Alcohol Abuse and Alcoholism (NIAAA)
6000 Executive Boulevard, Suite 409
Bethesda, MD 20892-7003
301-443-3860
http://www.niaaa.nih.gov

Parents' Resource Institute for Education (PRIDE)
3610 DeKalb Technology Parkway, Suite 105
Atlanta, GA 30340
770-458-9900
http://www.prideusa.org/

Students Against Driving Drunk (SADD)
P.O. Box 800
Marlboro, MA 01750
508-481-3568
http://www.sadd.org

Students to Offset Peer Pressure (STOPP)
P.O. Box 103, Department S
Hudson, NH 03051-0103

Agencies and Organizations in Canada

Addictions Foundation of Manitoba
1031 Portage Avenue
Winnipeg, Manitoba R3G 0R8
204-944-6277
http://www.mbnet.mb.ca/crm/
  health/afm.html

Addiction Research Foundation (ARF)
33 Russell Street
Toronto, Ontario M5S 2S1
416-595-6100
800-463-6273 in Ontario

Alberta Alcohol and Drug Abuse Commission

10909 Jasper Avenue, 6th Floor
Edmonton, Alberta T5J 3M9
http://www.gov.ab.ca/aadac/

British Columbia Prevention Resource Centre

96 East Broadway, Suite 211
Vancouver, British Columbia V5T 1V6
604-874-8452
800-663-1880 in British Columbia

Canadian Centre on Substance Abuse

75 Albert Street, Suite 300
Ottawa, Ontario K1P 5E7
613-235-4048
http://www.ccsa.ca/

Ontario Healthy Communities Central Office

180 Dundas Street West, Suite 1900
Toronto, Ontario M5G 1Z8
416-408-4841
http://www.opc.on.ca/ohcc/

Saskatchewan Health Resource Centre

T.C. Douglas Building
3475 Albert Street
Regina, Saskatchewan S4S 6X6
306-787-3090

Websites

Hazelden Foundation
http://www.hazelden.org/

Join Together Online (Substance Abuse)
http://www.jointogether.org/sa/

National Institute on Drug Abuse (NIDA)
http://www.nida.nih.gov

Partnership for a Drug-Free America
http://www.drugfreeamerica.org/

INDEX

Acetaldehyde, 18

Acetic acid, 18

Addiction. *See* Alcoholism

Advertising, 46, 59-61

Al-Anon, 33, 70

Alateen, 33, 70

Alcohol abuse, 16-17, 19, 48-49, 55-62, 66-68

Alcoholics Anonymous (AA), 32-33, 67, 69-70

Alcohol dehydrogenase (ADH), 18, 36

Alcoholic hepatitis, 42

Alcoholism, 13-16, 19, 24, 38, 39-40, 42, 43, 48, 49-53, 58, 59, 67, 68-71

Alcoholism: The Facts (Goodwin), 50

Alcoholism treatment, 69-70

Alcohol poisoning, 48

Alcohol Republic: An American Tradition, The (Rorabaugh), 24-25

Antabuse, 70

Barrymore, Drew, 13, 48

Beer, 20, 46, 56, 59, 61

Binge drinking, 56

Blood alcohol concentration (BAC), 20, 36-38

Brain, the, 18, 19, 22, 36, 38-40, 51, 68

Breathalyzer test, 36-37

Capote, Truman, 38

Chronic drinkers, 22-23

Cirrhosis, 42

Diabetes, 23, 24, 52

Digestion, 35-36, 42-43

Drunk driving, 17, 18-19, 24, 36-37, 38-39, 49, 60, 62-63, 65, 68

Eighteenth Amendment, 32

Enzymes, 18, 22-23, 36

Fatty liver, 41, 42

Good News About Drugs and Alcohol, The (Gold), 49-50

Gordis, Enoch, 51-52, 53

Heyman, Richard, 56, 61

Intoxication, 17, 20-22, 30, 38-39, 46, 47-48, 56

Kidneys, 36, 40, 42

Liver, the, 22-23, 36, 40-42

McGovern, George, 13-15

McGovern, Teresa Jane, 14-15

Metabolism, 35, 36, 40, 47, 48

Moderate drinking, 17-19, 28, 30, 49

Mothers Against Drunk Driving (MADD), 62

National Institute on Alcohol and Alcoholism (NIAAA), 16, 51, 59

Oxidation, 35-36

Peer pressure, 59-61, 65

Prohibition, 31, 32

Relapsing, 68-69

Rome, ancient, 28-29
Rush, Benjamin, 30

Shalala, Donna E., 59
Smith, Bob, 32
Social drinking, 19, 21
Students Against Driving Drunk
    (SADD), 62-63

Tolerance, 16, 19-23, 49

Twelve Steps Program, the, 33, 69-
    70

Underage drinking, 55-62

Washington, George, 30
Whiskey, 29, 30
Wilson, Bill, 32
Wine, 20, 46, 59
Withdrawal, 16, 68, 70

PICTURE CREDITS

NANCY PEACOCK is a freelance writer living in Medina, Ohio. She has written several travel books and one historical novel. Her articles and columns have appeared in *BusinessWeek, New Choices, Midwest Living, Romantic Homes, Cleveland Magazine,* and many other periodicals. She is also the author of *Drowning Our Sorrows: Psychological Effects of Alcohol Abuse* (1999) for Chelsea House Publishers.

BARRY R. McCAFFREY is Director of the Office of National Drug Control Policy (ONDCP) at the White House and a member of President Bill Clinton's cabinet. Before taking this job, General McCaffrey was an officer in the U.S. Army. He led the famous "left hook" maneuver of Operation Desert Storm that helped the United States win the Persian Gulf War.

STEVEN L. JAFFE, M.D., received his psychiatry training at Harvard University and the Massachusetts Mental Health Center and his child psychiatry training at Emory University. He has been editor of the *Newsletter of the American Academy of Child and Adolescent Psychiatry* and chairman of the Continuing Education Committee of the Georgia Psychiatric Physicians' Association. Dr. Jaffe is professor of child and adolescent psychiatry at Emory University. He is also clinical professor of psychiatry at Morehouse School of Medicine, and the director of Adolescent Substance Abuse Programs at Charter Peachford Hospital in Atlanta, Georgia.